A crafty way to color!

Enjoy this new way for colorists, cross stitchers, needle-pointers and embroiderers to relax, craft and create without a needle.

Grab some markers or pencils and follow the key with colors on these pages filled with the cutest halloween designs, from spooktacular ghosts to adorable wizard frogs, candy, kitties and so much more! It's similar to color by numbers but reminiscent of a counted cross stitch chart.

Use the key as a guide, but don't worry if you don't have all of the same colors! Use a dark magenta instead of a maroon if that's what you have available. Relax and enjoy the differences in your finished pages.

We recommend starting at the back of the book if you are using alcohol markers that bleed through the paper; placing some paper between the coloring pages as you go. The key on each page lists just the colors you will need, to help you prep for the page. The symbols are the same throughout the book for each color. There is a full key on the color testing page should you need it.

This book is also available in a Color by Number Mosaic version.

All rights reserved. No part of this book may be reproduced without written permission of the copyright owner.

Spelling it out

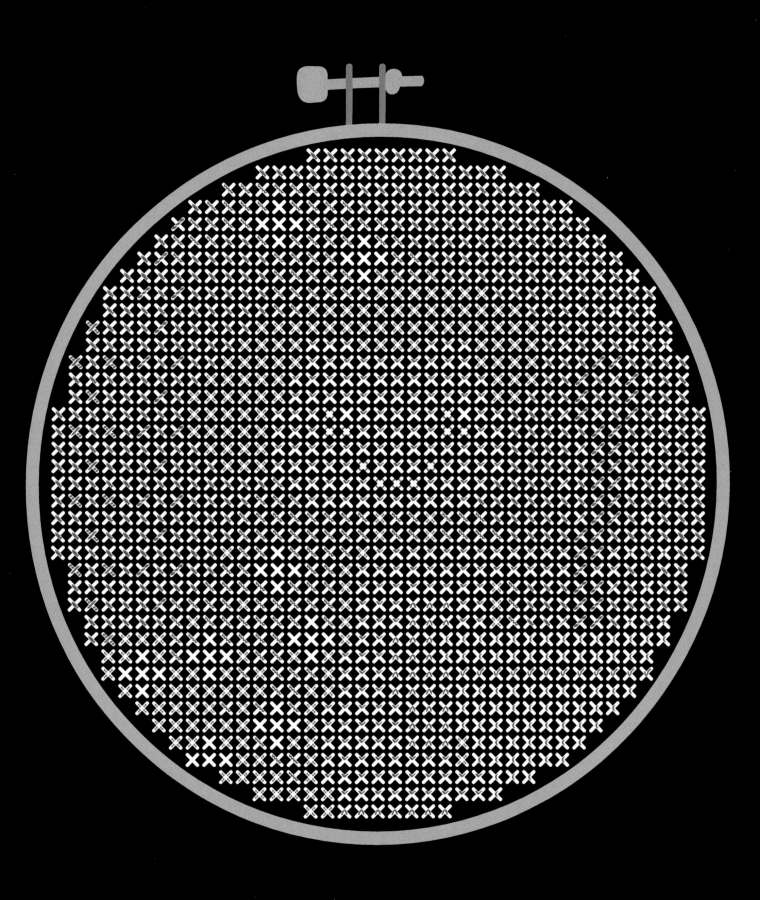

kitty
reaper

KEY

✖ black

✖ teal

✖ light yellow

✖ pink

✖ magenta

✖ purple

✖ light purple

✖ light gray

✖ charcoal

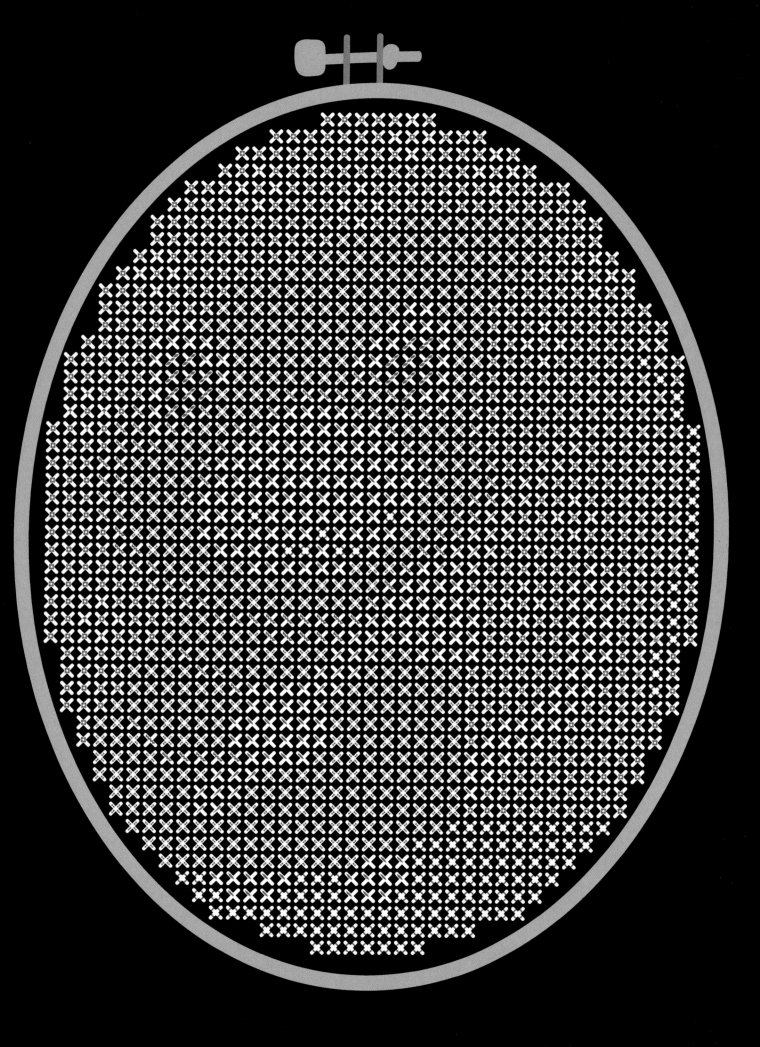

Quiet reading time

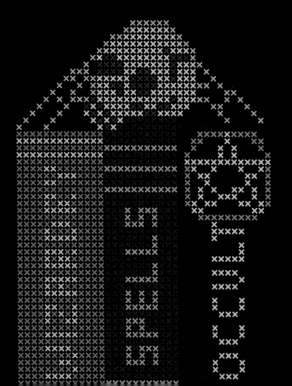

KEY

- ✖ navy
- ✖ **light blue**
- ✖ **light green**
- ✖ green
- ✖ orange
- ✖ maroon
- ✖ purple
- ✖ **light purple**
- ✖ **light gray**
- ✖ charcoal

Trick or treaty

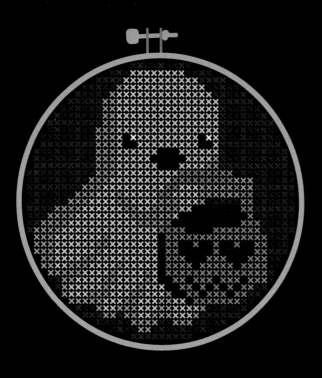

KEY
- ✖ black
- ✖ light blue
- ✖ teal
- ✖ red
- ✖ maroon
- ✖ purple
- ✖ light purple
- ✖ white

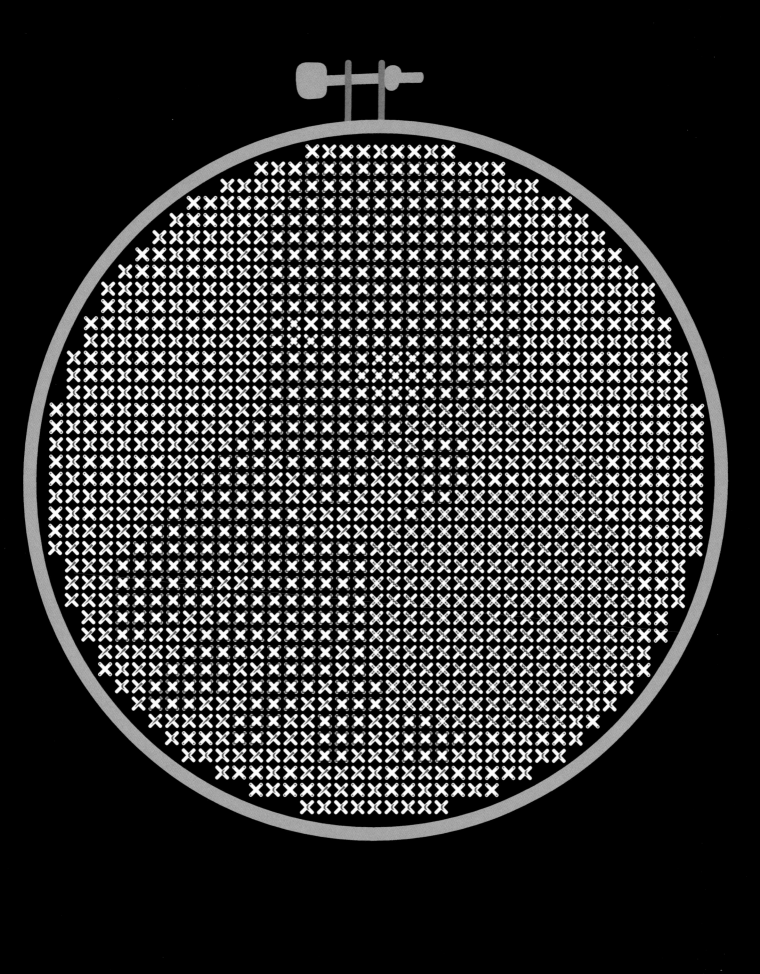

Skellycat snacks

KEY
× light blue
× light green
× pink
× red

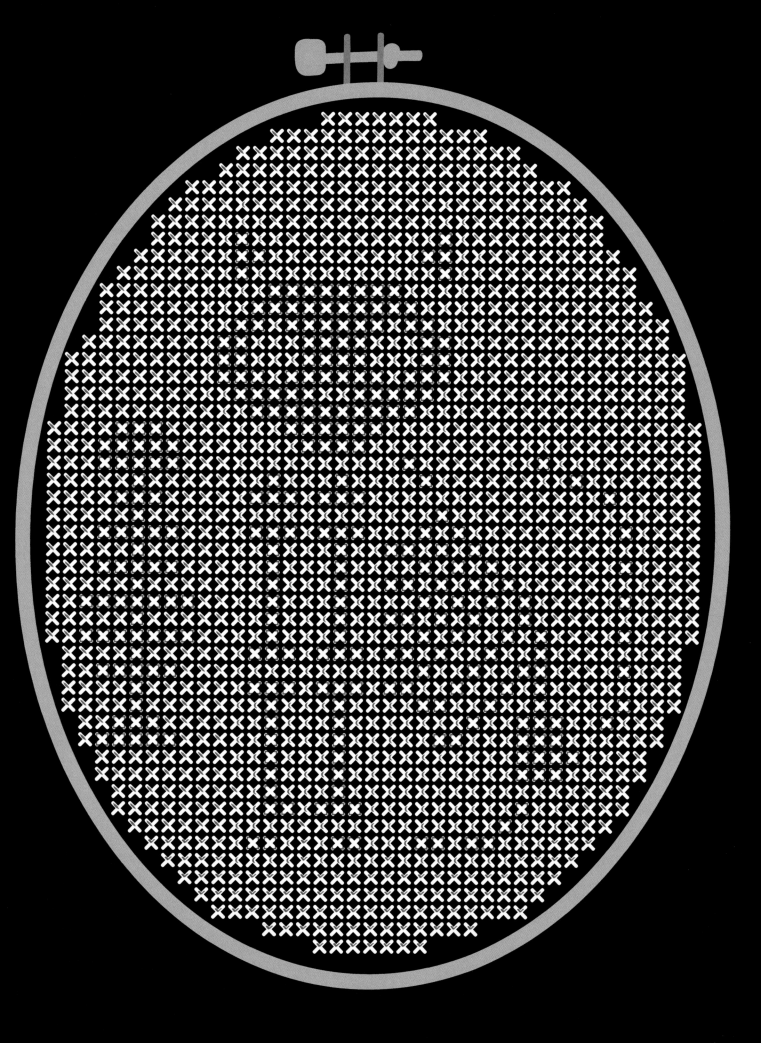

Finishing as I start

KEY

- ✕ black
- ✕ light green
- ✕ green
- ✕ orange
- ✕ dark orange
- ✕ light tan
- ✕ pink
- ✕ red
- ✕ maroon

Froggy flight

KEY

✗ black
✗ navy
✗ light green
✗ green
✗ yellow
✗ dark brown
✗ mid brown
✗ light gray
✗ charcoal
✗ white

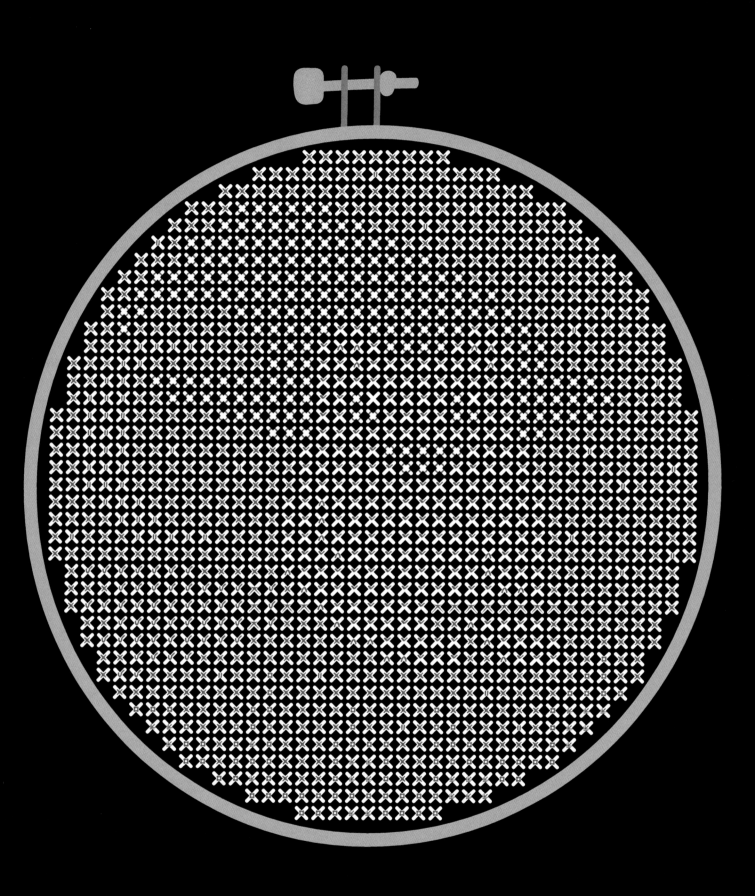

Skull or scull?

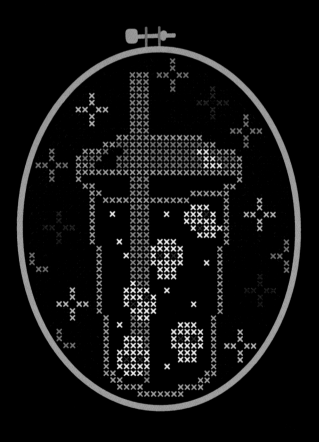

KEY

- ✖ black
- ✖ light blue
- ✖ orange
- ✖ magenta
- ✖ purple
- ✖ light purple
- ✖ light gray
- ✖ charcoal
- ✖ white

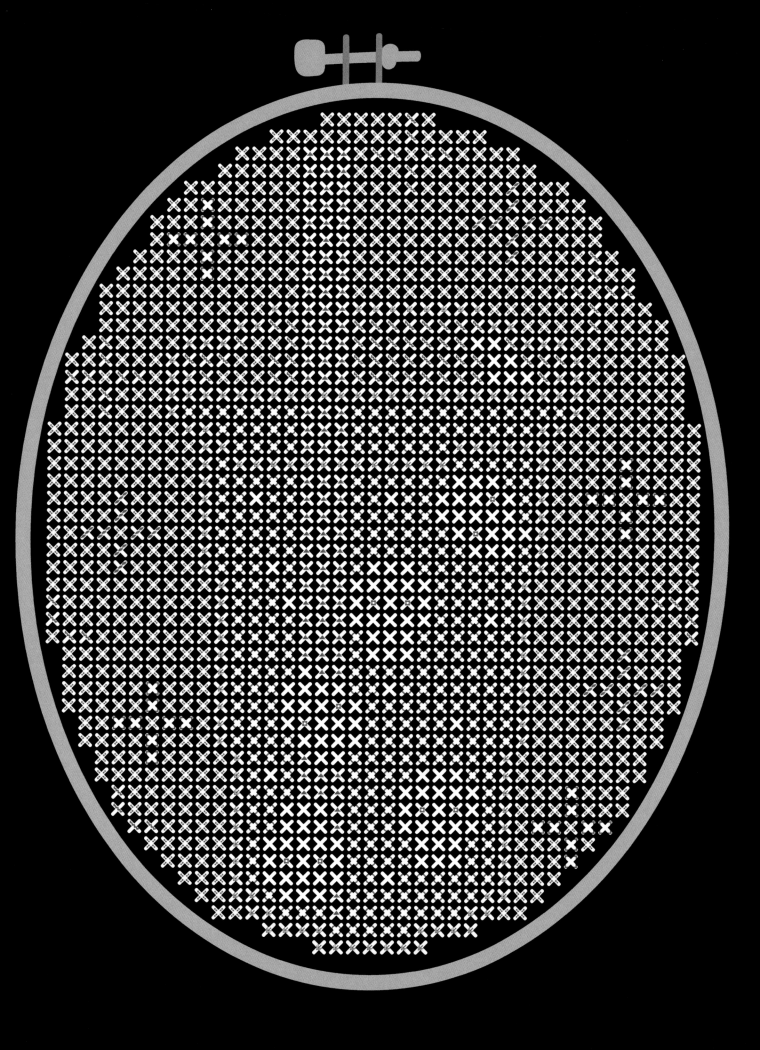

Heart of silk

KEY

- ✖ black
- ✖ light blue
- ✖ teal
- ✖ light green
- ✖ light yellow
- ✖ peach
- ✖ pink
- ✖ magenta
- ✖ light purple

Candy corn mouse

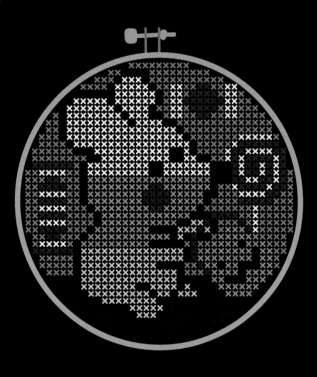

KEY

✖ black

✖ yellow

✖ orange

✖ magenta

✖ purple

✖ light purple

✖ white

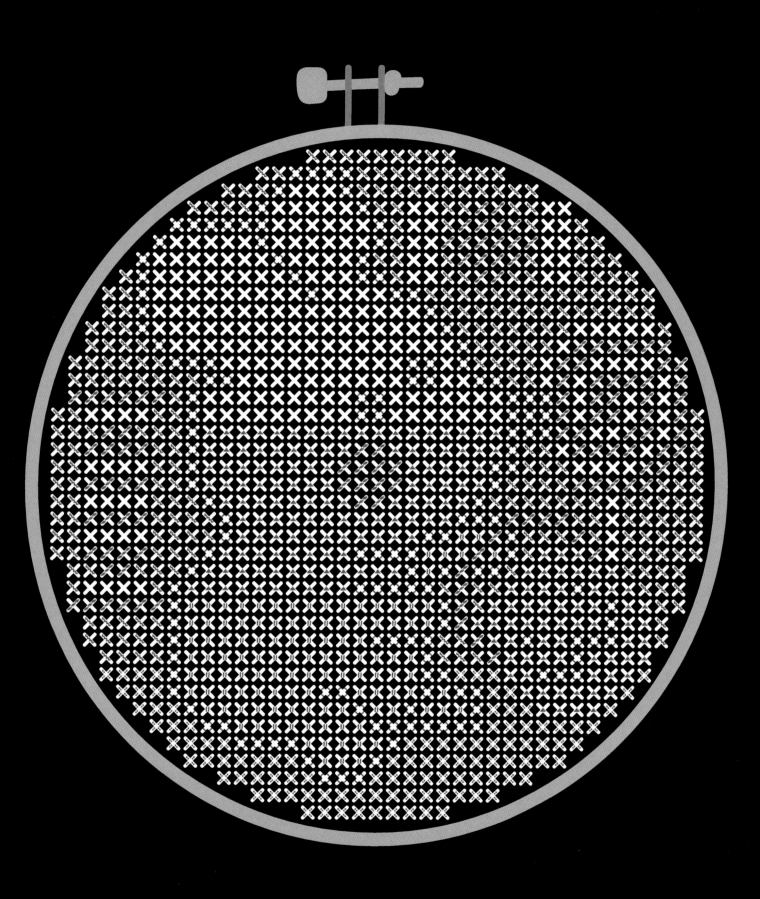

Candy roll

KEY

✖ black

✖ light blue

✖ teal

✖ light green

✖ peach

✖ pink

✖ purple

✖ light purple

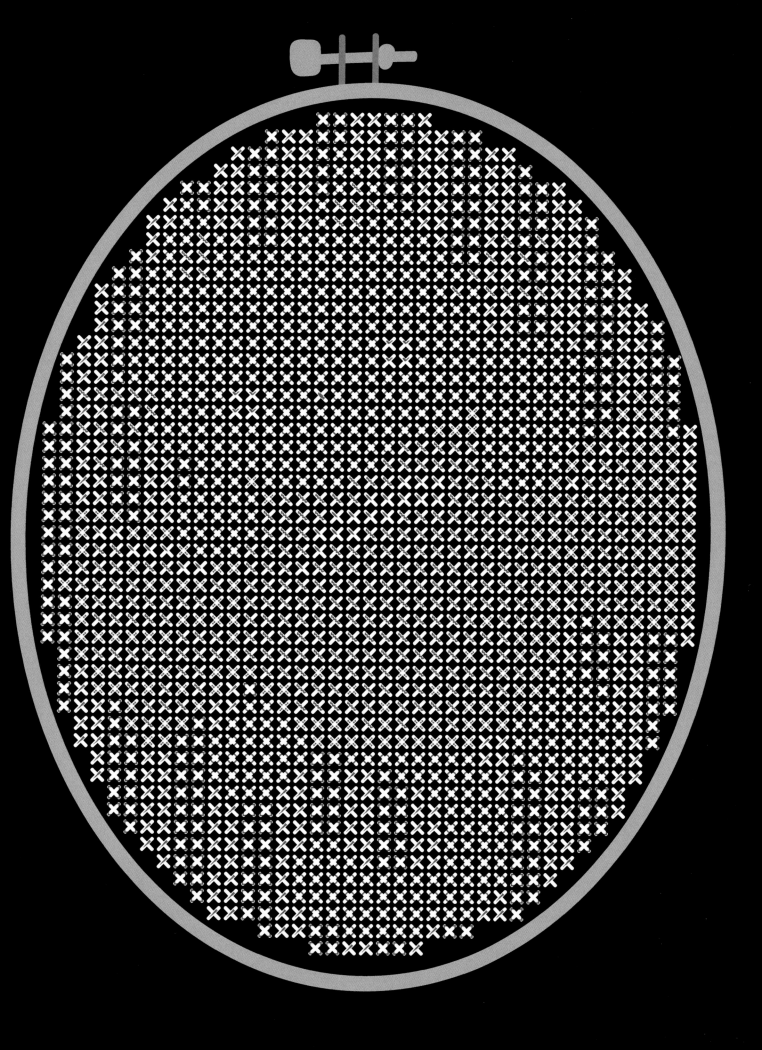

Sticky & sweet

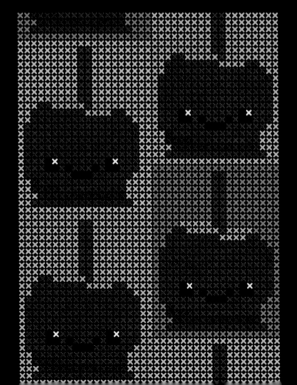

KEY

- ✖ black
- ✖ light blue
- ✖ light green
- ✖ dark brown
- ✖ pink
- ✖ red
- ✖ maroon
- ✖ light purple
- ✖ white

Vampire pumpkin

KEY

✗ black

✗ light green

✗ green

✗ light tan

✗ maroon

✗ purple

✗ light purple

✗ white

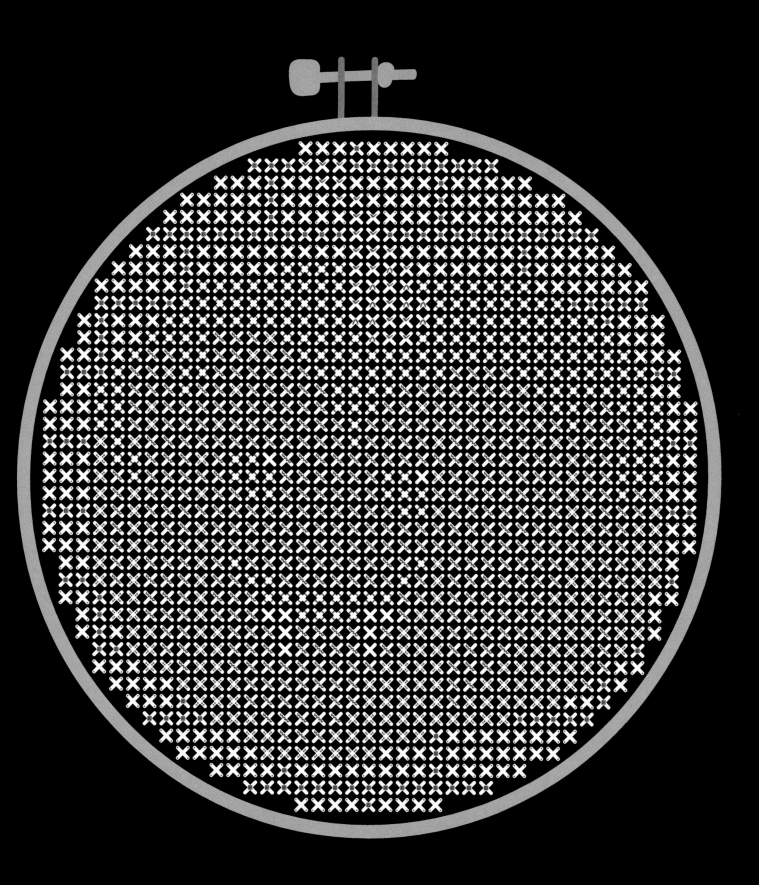

Witch's star-dome

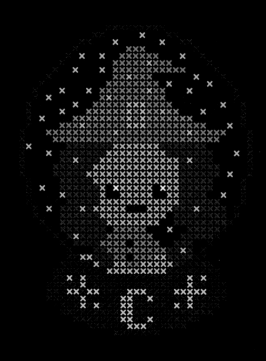

KEY

✕ black

✕ blue

✕ light blue

✕ light green

✕ yellow

✕ orange

✕ pink

✕ red

✕ light purple

✕ white

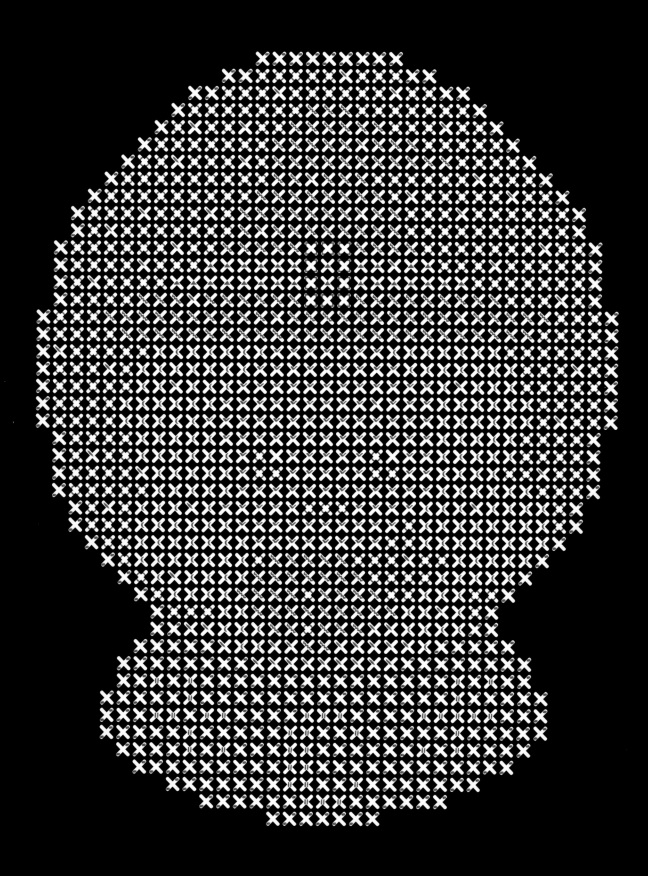

Boo's cruise

KEY

✕ black

✕ blue

✕ **light blue**

✕ dark orange

✕ **light tan**

✕ red

✕ purple

✕ **light purple**

✕ charcoal

✕ **white**

Wee zombie

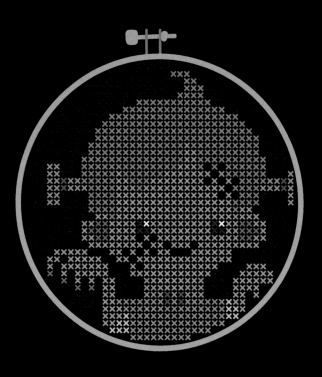

KEY

✖ black

✖ navy

✖ teal

✖ green

✖ orange

✖ dark orange

✖ mid brown

✖ light tan

✖ red

✖ light purple

✖ white

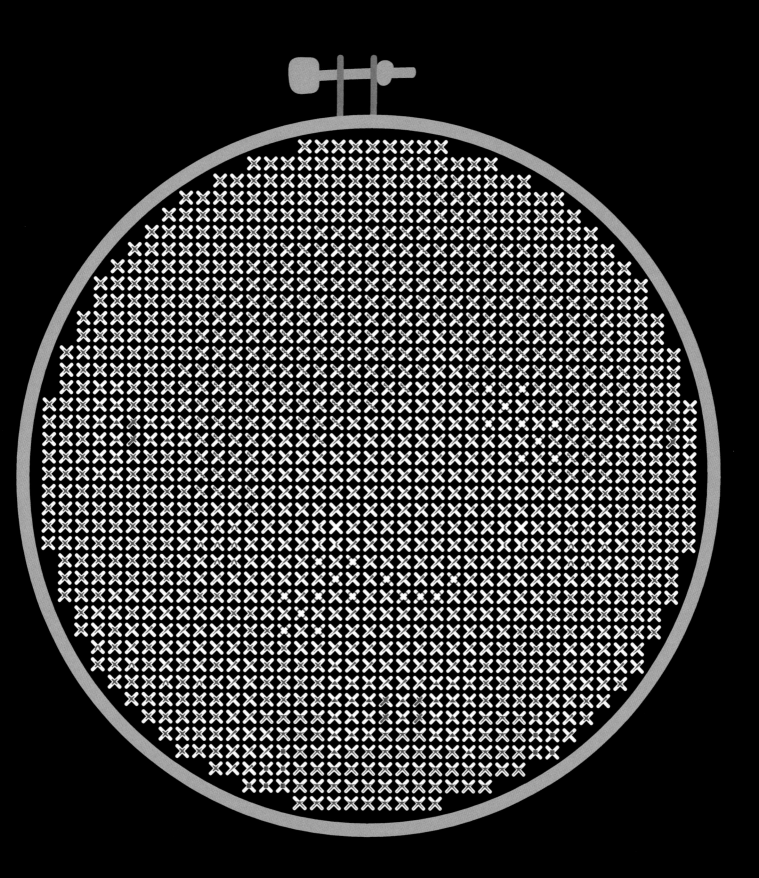

Dino might

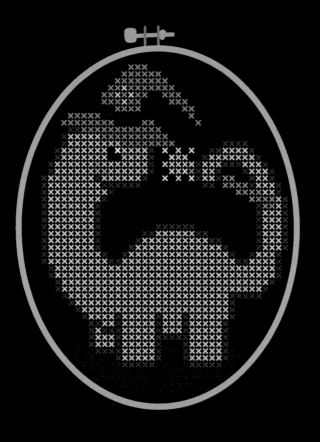

KEY

✕ black

✕ light blue

✕ light yellow

✕ yellow

✕ peach

✕ mid brown

✕ purple

✕ light purple

✕ charcoal

✕ white

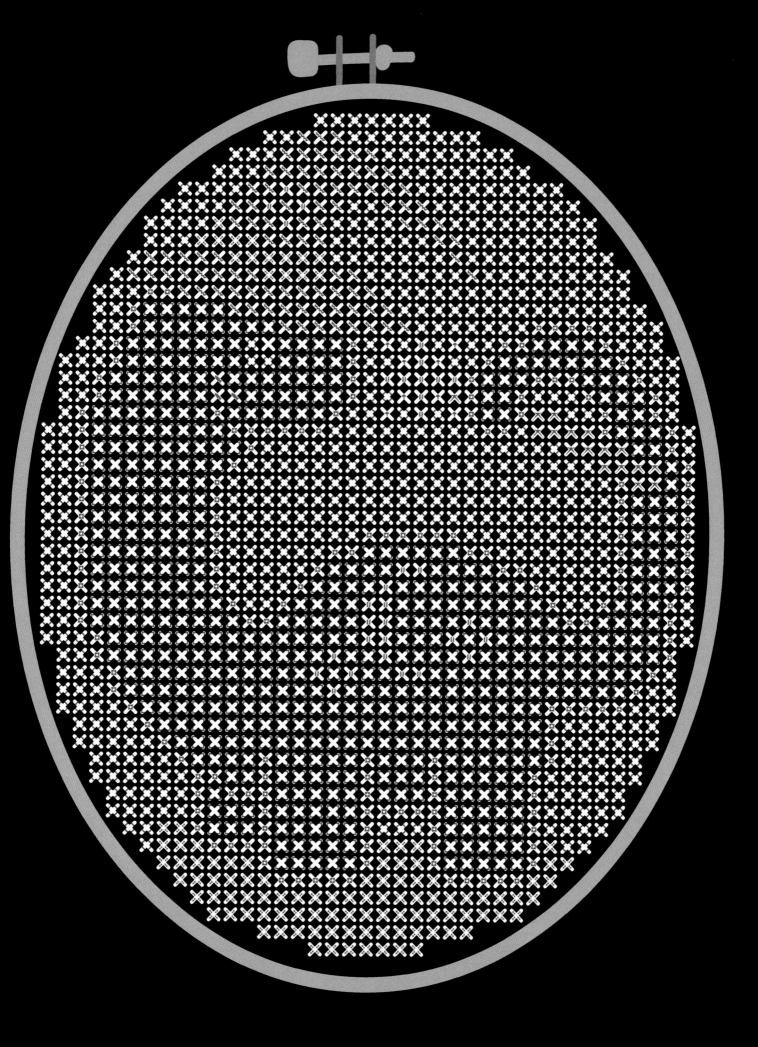

Full moon flight

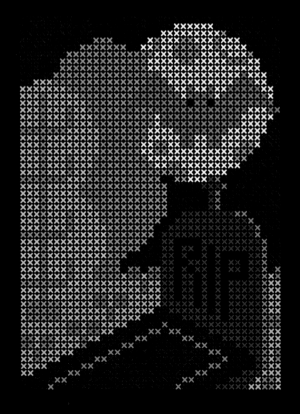

KEY

✖ black

✖ light blue

✖ teal

✖ light green

✖ orange

✖ purple

✖ light purple

✖ light gray

✖ mid gray

✖ charcoal

✖ white

Eye put a spell on you

KEY

✕ black

✕ navy

✕ light blue

✕ light green

✕ yellow

✕ peach

✕ orange

✕ purple

✕ light purple

✕ white

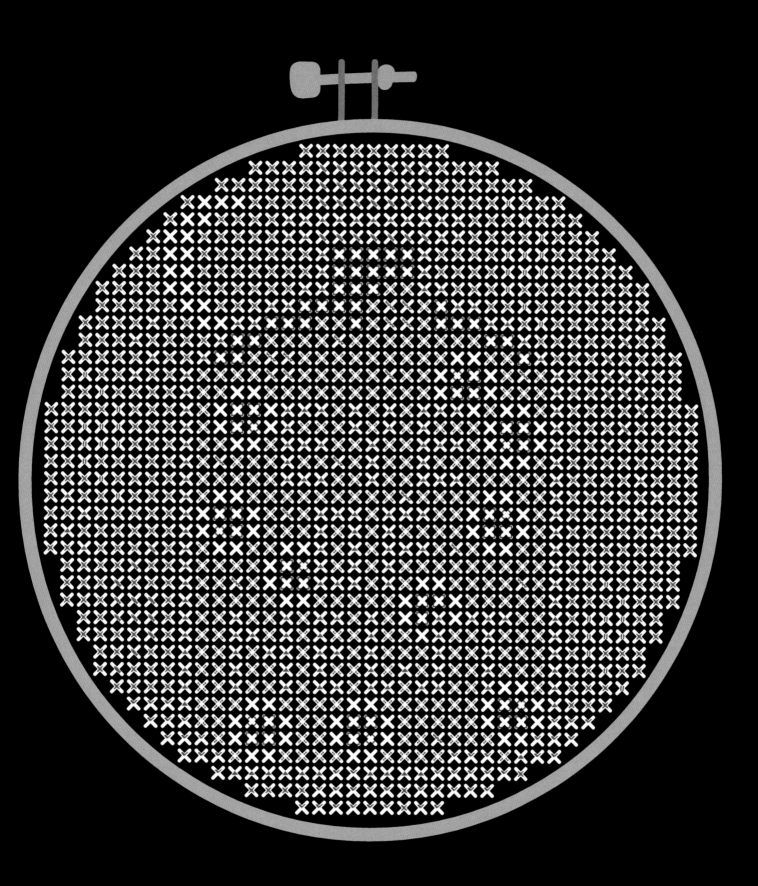

color test page

KEY

✗ black
✗ navy
✗ blue
✗ light blue
✗ teal
✗ light green
✗ green
✗ light yellow
✗ yellow
✗ peach
✗ orange
✗ dark orange
✗ dark brown
✗ mid brown
✗ light tan
✗ pink
✗ red
✗ magenta
✗ maroon
✗ purple
✗ light purple
✗ light gray
✗ mid gray
✗ charcoal
✗ white

What's your favorite Alice Mills style book?

Are you hooked on Cross Stitch Style Color by Symbol or has Mosaic Color by Number stolen your heart?

Cross Stitch Style Color by Symbol series
featuring premium paper ideal for alcohol or water based markers

Adorable Nature
CROSS STITCH STYLE
ADULT COLORING BOOK
ALICE MILLS PUBLISHING · PREMIUM PAPER EDITION

Christmas Delights
CROSS STITCH STYLE
ADULT COLORING BOOK
ALICE MILLS PUBLISHING · PREMIUM PAPER EDITION

Fantastic Flowers
CROSS STITCH STYLE
ADULT COLORING BOOK
ALICE MILLS PUBLISHING · PREMIUM PAPER EDITION

City Dreams
CROSS STITCH STYLE
ADULT COLORING BOOK
ALICE MILLS PUBLISHING · PREMIUM PAPER EDITION

Fantastic Folk Art
CROSS STITCH STYLE
ADULT COLORING BOOK
ALICE MILLS PUBLISHING · PREMIUM PAPER EDITION

Geometrical Joys
CROSS STITCH STYLE
ADULT COLORING BOOK
ALICE MILLS PUBLISHING · PREMIUM PAPER EDITION

Living Landscapes
CROSS STITCH STYLE
ADULT COLORING BOOK
ALICE MILLS PUBLISHING · PREMIUM PAPER EDITION

Halloween Spooks
CROSS STITCH STYLE
ADULT COLORING BOOK
ALICE MILLS PUBLISHING · PREMIUM PAPER EDITION

Vintage Tattoo Designs
CROSS STITCH STYLE
ADULT COLORING BOOK
ALICE MILLS PUBLISHING · PREMIUM PAPER EDITION

Kawaii Cuties
CROSS STITCH STYLE
ADULT COLORING BOOK
ALICE MILLS PUBLISHING · PREMIUM PAPER EDITION

Frosted Cookies & Cakes
CROSS STITCH STYLE
ADULT COLORING BOOK
ALICE MILLS PUBLISHING · PREMIUM PAPER EDITION

Magical Marine Life
CROSS STITCH STYLE
ADULT COLORING BOOK
ALICE MILLS PUBLISHING · PREMIUM PAPER EDITION

Blissful Summer Days
CROSS STITCH STYLE
ADULT COLORING BOOK
ALICE MILLS PUBLISHING · PREMIUM PAPER EDITION

Sweetest Blooms
CROSS STITCH STYLE
ADULT COLORING BOOK
ALICE MILLS PUBLISHING · PREMIUM PAPER EDITION

Magical Forest Folk
CROSS STITCH STYLE
ADULT COLORING BOOK
ALICE MILLS PUBLISHING · PREMIUM PAPER EDITION

Enchanting Fantasy
CROSS STITCH STYLE
ADULT COLORING BOOK
ALICE MILLS PUBLISHING · PREMIUM PAPER EDITION

Bottled Treasures
CROSS STITCH STYLE
ADULT COLORING BOOK
ALICE MILLS PUBLISHING · PREMIUM PAPER EDITION

Cutest Christmas
CROSS STITCH STYLE
ADULT COLORING BOOK

Kawaii Pets
CROSS STITCH STYLE
ADULT COLORING BOOK
ALICE MILLS PUBLISHING · PREMIUM PAPER EDITION

Punchy Patterns
CROSS STITCH STYLE
ADULT COLORING BOOK
ALICE MILLS PUBLISHING · PREMIUM PAPER EDITION

Kawaii Halloween
CROSS STITCH STYLE
ADULT COLORING BOOK

Join us on Instagram where we share news and new releases with you.

 **@alicemillspublishing**

We hope you enjoyed this book! If you have the time to leave a review that would help us so much.

Mosaic Color by Number series
featuring premium paper ideal for alcohol or water based markers

Easter Fun!
MOSAIC COLOR BY NUMBER
ADULT COLORING BOOK
ALICE MILLS PUBLISHING · COLOR BY NUMBER SERIES · BOOK ONE

Dazzling Animals!
MOSAIC COLOR BY NUMBER
ADULT COLORING BOOK
ALICE MILLS PUBLISHING · COLOR BY NUMBER SERIES

Blissful Summer Days
MOSAIC COLOR BY NUMBER
ADULT COLORING BOOK
ALICE MILLS PUBLISHING · PREMIUM PAPER EDITION

Sweetest Blooms
MOSAIC COLOR BY NUMBER
ADULT COLORING BOOK
ALICE MILLS PUBLISHING · PREMIUM PAPER EDITION

Magical Forest Folk
MOSAIC COLOR BY NUMBER
ADULT COLORING BOOK
ALICE MILLS PUBLISHING · PREMIUM PAPER EDITION

Adorable Nature
MOSAIC COLOR BY NUMBER
ADULT COLORING BOOK
ALICE MILLS PUBLISHING · PREMIUM PAPER EDITION

Halloween Spooks
MOSAIC COLOR BY NUMBER
ADULT COLORING BOOK
ALICE MILLS PUBLISHING · PREMIUM PAPER EDITION

Christmas Delights
MOSAIC COLOR BY NUMBER
ADULT COLORING BOOK
ALICE MILLS PUBLISHING · PREMIUM PAPER EDITION

Frosted Cookies & Cakes
MOSAIC COLOR BY NUMBER
ADULT COLORING BOOK
ALICE MILLS PUBLISHING · PREMIUM PAPER EDITION

Kawaii Cuties
MOSAIC COLOR BY NUMBER
ADULT COLORING BOOK
ALICE MILLS PUBLISHING · PREMIUM PAPER EDITION

Geometrical Joys
MOSAIC COLOR BY NUMBER
ADULT COLORING BOOK
ALICE MILLS PUBLISHING · PREMIUM PAPER EDITION

Enchanting Fantasy
MOSAIC COLOR BY NUMBER
ADULT COLORING BOOK
ALICE MILLS PUBLISHING · PREMIUM PAPER EDITION

Fantastic Flowers
MOSAIC COLOR BY NUMBER
ADULT COLORING BOOK
ALICE MILLS PUBLISHING · PREMIUM PAPER EDITION

City Dreams
MOSAIC COLOR BY NUMBER
ADULT COLORING BOOK
ALICE MILLS PUBLISHING · PREMIUM PAPER EDITION

Fantastic Folk Art
MOSAIC COLOR BY NUMBER
ADULT COLORING BOOK
ALICE MILLS PUBLISHING · PREMIUM PAPER EDITION

Bottled Treasures
MOSAIC COLOR BY NUMBER
ADULT COLORING BOOK
ALICE MILLS PUBLISHING · PREMIUM PAPER EDITION

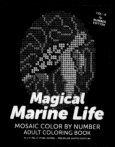

Magical Marine Life
MOSAIC COLOR BY NUMBER
ADULT COLORING BOOK
ALICE MILLS PUBLISHING · PREMIUM PAPER EDITION

Living Landscapes
MOSAIC COLOR BY NUMBER
ADULT COLORING BOOK
ALICE MILLS PUBLISHING · PREMIUM PAPER EDITION

Vintage Tattoo Designs
MOSAIC COLOR BY NUMBER
ADULT COLORING BOOK
ALICE MILLS PUBLISHING · PREMIUM PAPER EDITION

Cutest Christmas
MOSAIC COLOR BY NUMBER
ADULT COLORING BOOK
ALICE MILLS PUBLISHING · PREMIUM PAPER EDITION

Kawaii Pets
CROSS STITCH STYLE
ADULT COLORING BOOK
ALICE MILLS PUBLISHING · PREMIUM PAPER EDITION

Punchy Patterns
MOSAIC COLOR BY NUMBER
ADULT COLORING BOOK
ALICE MILLS PUBLISHING · PREMIUM PAPER EDITION

Kawaii Halloween
MOSAIC COLOR BY NUMBER
ADULT COLORING BOOK
ALICE MILLS PUBLISHING · PREMIUM PAPER EDITION

Made in the USA
Middletown, DE
08 June 2023

32271255R00024